AF580409

My Reflections

ADITYA

Published by ADITYA, 2024.

While every precaution has been taken in the preparation of this book, the publisher assumes no responsibility for errors or omissions, or for damages resulting from the use of the information contained herein.

MY REFLECTIONS

First edition. December 1, 2024.

Copyright © 2024 ADITYA.

ISBN: 979-8230310440

Written by ADITYA.

To mu loving parents,wife, kids and friends who make everything meaningful

Selective reflections

Our sweet words can do magic
Harsh words are like arrows
They create wounds forever
Sweet words are must for us
They give hope ,happiness
So we should be careful

Speech control

Uncontrolled and no social language is daily violence

If we believe in God we should never resort to uncontrolled use of speech

True knowledge lies in controlled use of speech

True follower of God never loose self control

Control of senses gives us happiness and peace

It is important that we honour each other and be sensitive towards circumstances

Even Sri Ram says my True devotees should control their senses

Patience

Don't get involved in unnecessary works ,that leads to mental problems

Don't expect people to praise u everywhere

He thinks Everyone is brainless,and they should do as I say

We should follow great saints who have controlled their mind and senses

We don't need to oppress ourselves ,we need to channelise our energies

A person who controls his senses cannot be violent

Speaking and eating whole day is bad

Speech violence

Such a person can never be at peace
Due to mental imbalance he will critise even good deeds
Some keep on doing self praise and keep on critising others
Civilized society laughs on such persons
We should not have caste,creed,money discrimination
Our words should not hurt anyone
So mind ,speech control leads to a happy person,happy society

My Grandmother

Wherever we are
I will reach for u,I will remember u
And I know I will find ur touch everywhere
There is a part of u in everything I do
But the smile I knew no longer waits there
They say there is a road to where u are
It's not on the map,but it can't be too far
If u have gone to stay ,there must be a way to where u r
Love is the way to where u r
A shower of light ,a rainbow of tears
Our love is a prayer,blessing us
Wherever u r

True love

work of mirroring and magnifying each other

Facts vs faction

If something is inconvenient and uncomfortable we usually ignore it

We distort truth just to suit us

We usually become selective about information

Will such distortion of truth stay for ever

I think a day comes when factions can also be uncomfortably prickly when they r exposed

Compassion

U r not helping anyone
No one is healer
Noone is wounded
We have to be Equals
Unless we realize our own suffering ,we can't really help anyone
To remove darkness,we need to experience our own sad moments
That is true humanity

Wisdom search

Do we need special places for self realization
Just open your eyes
Nature teaches us everywhere
Just be open and willing to pause
Like bees visit many flowers,but honey is one
So we need to rise into a higher way of thinking
We can lead a more harmonious life

Spirituality

Web of Worldly Affairs,goals,wealth,
possessions stucks all of us
Is only sensory experience real
Will only material gains give us peace and contentment
Material things have a temporary nature
Spiritual path is only way back to God
Most important is not to get attached to them
Meditation helps us to move our attention from outer world to the inner world

Then we get **love, joy,happiness**
This is a way to realise God in our life
We will get happiness and joy
We can assess our private inner retreat by meditation
It removes all stress and strains
All eternity is in the moment
Death is certain for the born
Rebirth is inevitable for the dead
We should not grieve for inevitable
Existence is a brief pause between manifest and unmanifest

Material things

God has given us so much

It is our responsibility to use these for our spiritual progress

We Don't need to stop using material things

Problem starts when we think getting these things to be the only purpose of life

This leads to stress,sadness

We should not spend whole life just to accumulate these things

At the end we have to leave these things

So do not get lost in never ending desires

Work life balance

Some say their work is their relaxation
In evening Mind has to take a meaningful break
Detach psychologically from work
Practice mindfulness
Can practice evening sandhya
Engage mind and train it to stay engaged
We can profit from humanity treasure trove of knowledge
To be calm is one the greatest asset in the world

Pride is the biggest enemy

We can defeat pride

Philosophy are the questions that may never be answered

Religion are the answers that must never be questioned

Philosophy is a luxury for few ,religion is a consolation for the many

Forgiving

Forgiving is only way to get our own peace

We must learn to live life with depth and peacefully

If we **define the problem correctly**,you almost have the solution

How to avoid loneliness,depression,sorrow

Most important key to happiness is intellect

Intellect gives us ability to find truth

We need to look in

We need to shift our gaze from world to ourself

We need to change the way we think,feel and act

We need to enjoy instant pleasure,also invest in our long term happiness

Work in a spirit of yajna,service and

<u>sacrifice</u> for a higher ideal

All unselfish people are happy

Expand your circle,feel one with people

Experience incredible result of collective,cooperative effort

The larger the circle of love,the greater the happiness

Importance of proper speech

Sometimes we are not able to express ourselves properly

If we say bad words we get punished

If we say good words we get happiness

If we hurt someone,he always remembers

Be careful when we **use words**

It should not pierce someone's heart

Quest for joy

We all are seekers

Life needs intuition

Life cannot be solved with logic and reason alone

Actions must be aligned with our highest values and purpose

Power from work

Lots of people give their best in office

Some don't work properly and try to do incomplete work

We should give our best

We must realize our responsibility

We might feel discouraged when less hard working people are given equal weightage

Work is life

Better human

All are same
We Should respect humanity
Don't do any work to hurt anyone
Help neighbors
All trials to be done to help all
Forgiving
It takes us forward
Be patient and forgive everyone
If we do wrong we should apologise

Be gentle

Happiness

We all have different notions of happiness

Happiness is a mind set

Discipline ur mind and body

Find out root cause of problem and try to correct it

Hate the sin,love the sinner

Overcome anger with compassion

Overcome violence with love

Free your mind

Never get brainwashed into believing what others say about you

We keep on changing

Our mind is a meeting place for various natural forces,desires,fears

Our ancestors play a big role in shaping what we become

We should pay our debts as laid down by shastras

Discipline is most important link between our planning and our goal

Freedom from hatred

Whole world is full of **hatred**

Mutual respect and respect is lacking
Hatred vanishes love,empathy
We miss true values
If we love something we can't see faults in that thing
If we hate something we can't see goodness in that person.
World constantly changes,we should not consider it Stationary
If we hate someone we cannot get positive results

To become great we need to give to earth

We must **use our energy properly**
Then only God will love and bless us
God has given us power,brain,skills,good qualities
We don't recognise these skills
We misuse these powers
Our aim is to correctly use our powers
We must recognise our life meaning
Then whole world will have happiness,peace,prosperity

Defeat

It makes us beautiful
When we suffer we become better
Then only we find our way out of the depths
We must have sensitivity ,compassion
The demon is always within
The Goddess is also always within
We fight our battles within
Who wins,demon or God that choice is also always within

Time Importance

Time is so important in life
    Hard work at right time is very important
    True value of any work dependence whether it is done at right time or not
    We should not keep on postponing work
    If we do this time will pass off
    And then even if we do work in haste we will not get benefits
    If we do work at right time then only we can get quality

Harmony

It is so important
Harmony between body and soul nourishes us
Harmony between individuals is equally important
So many tragedies in world can be avoided if we have Harmony
Sometimes we don't accept others viewpoints
This leads to indifference between people
We should respect and accommodate all ideas and views

We should not be **judgemental**

We hastly form opinions and take decisions
Usually we look at negative side of anything
So truth changes
Our heart should accept all
We all can be right
Every individual has a right of freedom of expression and worship
There is always a possibility that even our opponents may be right
Every belief can fit in mankind

Words

Words are biggest power in this world
They are biggest weapons and also biggest medicine
So they have both positive and negative energy in them
So we need to be careful when we use them
Words have lot of importance
Transformation of Words into language is true visualization of God

Knowledge of right and wrong

Balance is so important

Everywhere everyone is running for their own recognition
We all strive for independence by money,beauty,brains,behavior
We have so many delusions
We should strive for balance
This comes from good character
Character is meditation
What we achieve by good character that is permanent

We all are surrounded by lots of problems

Biggest problem is unbalanced growth
These all are blind alleys
It is so difficult to come out of these alleys
We should not forget morality
True growth is possible only by healthy lifestyle
Don't go by just what everyone is doing
We may have less growth,but our happiness is very important
Even if we face adversities then too we should help others

Our weakness

Brains are more important than power

Proper policies are so important

We should progress on road of religiousness,love,devotion

We should accept our weakness

We should pray for happiness,health for all

We should try to form bridges between different divisions of society

It is so easy to cure a physical disease

Mental health is even more important

We cannot see mental problems just like physical problems
Society also leave such people alone
This loneliness makes mental diseases even bigger burden
Person must understand his problem and express it
Otherwise he will keep on suffering
We need to find ourselves
We can't just keep on hiding
We need to take steps

Laziness

We all want success

All don't do hard work for success

Laziness means to keep on postponing,not doing work on right time

Time is so precious

Laziness destroys time

Lazy person cannot achieve anything

This affects that person,society, nation

We should be disciplined in our daily routine

We should clearly relate to our life aim

Time management and ideal lifestyle is important

Mental health

This is one of the biggest concerns

Kf we don't get right direction ,aggression and depression can set in

Meditation and breathing is so important

Spirituality brings never ending happiness

The joy of giving is best

Sharing gives us happiness

It purifies our mind and brings immense joy
When we help others then God takes care of us
We should help without expecting any returns
These are to be done repeatedly
Just speaking about positive things purifies us
Best service is to uplift someone's state of mind

New mornings

Is it possible all goes well in life
We all start day with positive thoughts
We shouldn't blame time for all problems
Don't worry for past
Weak decisions harm us
True values shouldn't change
We need people who are ready to change
And we should give our best for change
Stay away from bad practices
We should not fear questions

We should fulfill our dreams

Don't blame destiny
Frame your own destiny
Ask questions from others as well as yourself
This is a way to reach your goals
And this is true morning for us
True good character
Our inner strength and truth are our biggest weapons
Give your full concentration and devotion to whatever we do

There is only one way for truth

Like Ravan has ten heads,so that lead to ten ways and confusion
We must be concentrated

Dusherra
Ego and darker impulses lead to our downfall
We must burn these bad characters
True victory lies in internal mastery of self
Universe will support us if we are true,righteous

We must shed ego,past deeds,false identities

This is important for spiritual growth

Remembrance of God

This helps to solve all problems and tensions

This is like a medicine

When a honest true heart prays to God,his prayers are always answered

So even ordinary people can solve their problems by praying to God

We should always complete our responsibilities

Constant remembrance provides many powers to us

Some time Should be spent in God remembrance
We all enjoy Worldly pleasures
We don't like to meditate
Unless we meditate from our heart ,it won't be of use

Allow nature to teach us stillness
Let our awareness rest upon a tree,plant,flower
How still they are,how deeply rooted in just being

Positive living

We should not look back
We should have a positive attitude
Inner divinity is our guide
We should not get carried away by emotions
We should keep on practicing detachment
Divine is within us
We should have good views for everyone
Then only respect,love can be there
So to change circumstances,we need to change views

Satisfaction

There is no end to our desires
No one is happy even if they get crores
But this affects our body and mind
So we accumulate even more than our needs
And our mind cannot rest
So to satisfy mind we keep on working
We need to realize limits of satisfaction
Keep on working but don't exhaust yourself

We think Spirituality is needed when we grow old

It is totally opposite

Main aim of Spirituality is to live with freedom and fulfilment

It helps us to Overcome our mind and intelligence

It free us from slavery of objects and circumstances

Spirituality begins where religion ends

Why do we search for creator

We try to find reason for universe Existence

Ultimate reality has to transcend duality

We should shift focus to our deepest core

We need to discover truth of our identity
Our life is full of complexities
We all have different minds,qualities
We have to choose our own path
If we depend on others it will lead to confusion
Decisions should be based on our own understanding
If our path is based on others opinions it can neer give us happiness
This increases our confidence

Problems are bound to come

When we take our own decisions it increases our self confidence

Our shortcomings are our greatest teacher

That is best way to improve

We must listen to our inner voice

Final decision should always be based on our own experiences

This makes life meaningful

This is the reason that no one can understand us more than ourselves

Struggle

Sometimes we have to struggle in life
That too special struggle
We have to do something special
This tests our patience
We will get success by patience
Even when a diya knows it's dark all around then too it keeps on spreading light
Darkness may be powerful
Then too diya never looses patience
Even darkness doesn't dares to enter premises of diya

Diya fights his own battle

He never expects help from anyone
He doesn't cry
He know to save his existence he has to fight
If he ceases to fight then darkness will swallow him
So diya defeats darkness
We should accept truth of struggle in our life
When we fight then we create history
We should face life with smile,then we can experience life

Good at heart

Your good behaviors and thoughts spread around like a perfume
If a good person protests about wrong things then change happens
A true person respects and cares for all humans
We have great books like Gita
We need to activate goodness in our hearts to protect our society
For building a good nation good virtues are important

Don't miss out!

Visit the website below and you can sign up to receive emails whenever ADITYA publishes a new book. There's no charge and no obligation.

https://books2read.com/r/B-A-WFPXC-MCNJF

BOOKS 2 READ

Connecting independent readers to independent writers.

About the Author

DR Aditya Mani Gupta is an orthopaedic surgeon.He has an interest in reading new infromation.He truly believes in sharing good information with everyone.

lets make this world a better place

Read more at dradityamani@gmail.com.

www.ingramcontent.com/pod-product-compliance
Lightning Source LLC
LaVergne TN
LVHW090124160826
845673LV00015B/842

* 9 7 9 8 2 3 0 3 1 0 4 4 0 *